KU-486-100

TONY HART

ART & CRAFT

GUILD PUBLISHING   LONDON

This edition published in 1984 by
Kaye & Ward Ltd
Copyright © 1983, 1984 Tony Hart
Reprinted 1985
All rights reserved. No part of this publication may be reproduced,
stored in a retrieval system, or transmitted in any form or by any
means, electronic, mechanical, photocopying, recording or otherwise,
without the permission of copyright owner.
Printed in Great Britain by Springbourne Press Ltd

Contents

BONE PICTURES

Bones can be made into interesting and unusual pictures. First you will need to collect some bones, but before you use them you must ask an adult to boil them in washing soda. After boiling the bones will be clean and white.

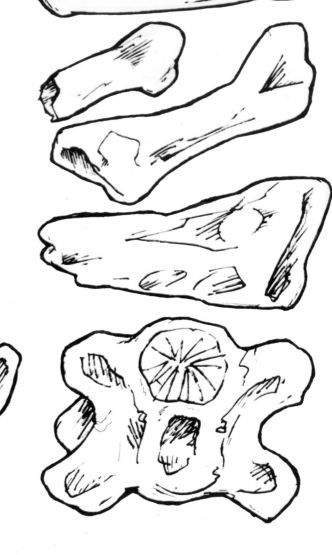

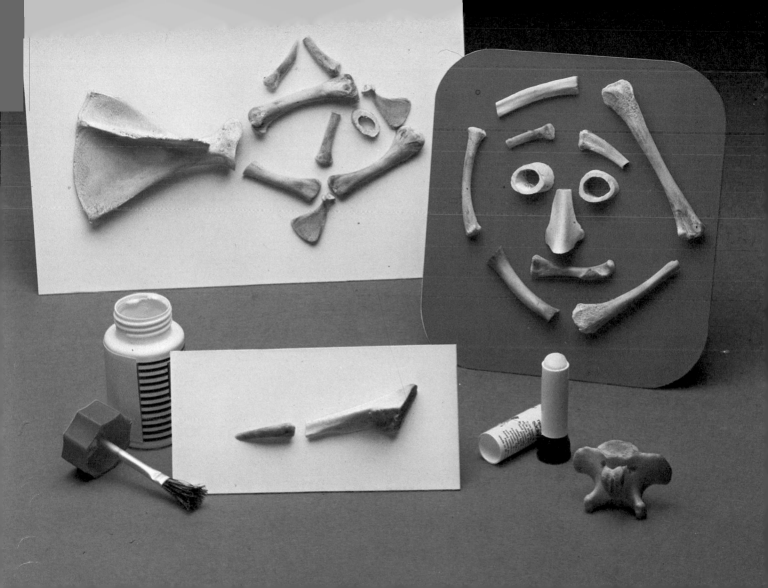

Arrange the bones into a picture onto a coloured card. Choose a colour that shows up the bones well.

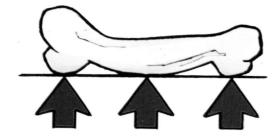

Note where each bone touches the background and apply glue to these places. Stick the bone onto the card.

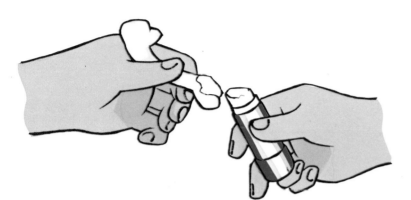

Glue all the bones on the card in this way. Try making bone pictures on different types of background like wood, material or coloured paper.

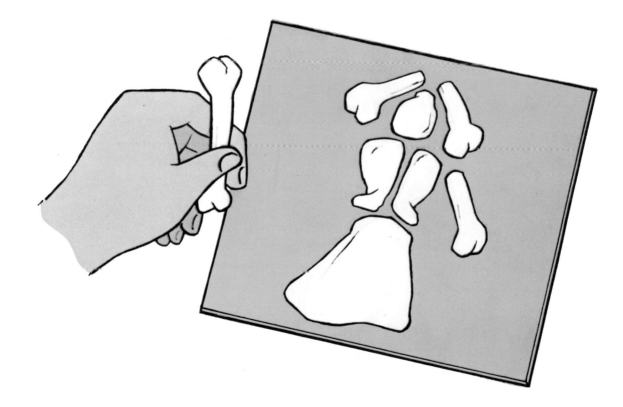

PET STONES

You can make lots of animals and figures from stones. Wash the stones first to remove mud or gravel.

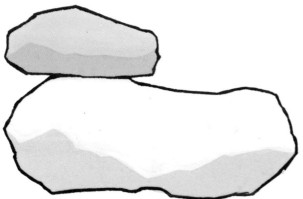

Experiment with the stones until you make a shape that you like. They should balance in position to make gluing easier. Use a glue stick.

Make different expressions by using different shaped eyes and large or small pupils.

STRAW HORSE. To make the body of a horse gather a bundle of straw 40 mm across by 150 mm long.

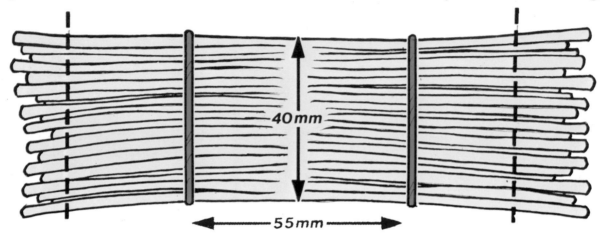

40mm

55mm

Tie the bundle in two places 55 mm apart, using cotton or thin wire. Trim flat the ends of the bundle with scissors.

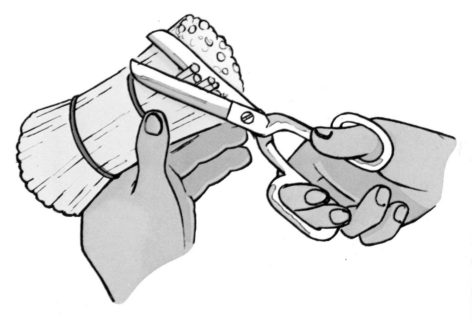

Make 4 legs in the same way as the body but using the dimensions shown here.

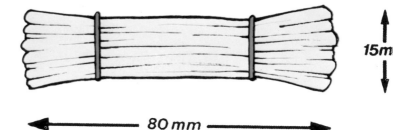

15m.

80 mm

Push 4 cocktail sticks into the body and push the legs onto these cocktail sticks. Make a tail by folding two or three pieces of straw in half and tying them tightly.

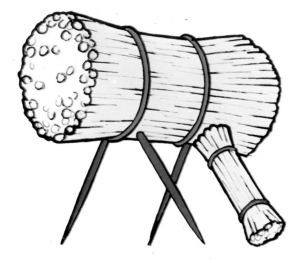

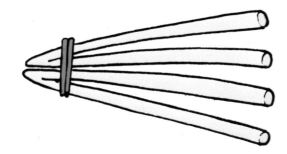

Push the tail into one end of the body.

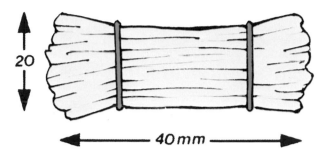

20

40 mm

Make a neck 40 mm long and 20 mm across.

Push another cocktail stick into the body and push the neck onto it, as shown.

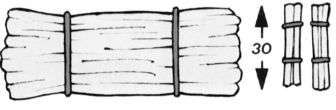

70

30

Make a head and ears to the size shown above.

Fix the head to the neck with a cocktail stick. Break another stick in half and use it to put the ears on.

WINDOW DECORATIONS

Put white kitchen tissue onto several sheets of newspaper. Use red, blue and yellow ink or thick poster paint and dab on the colours with a big brush or sponge until you have covered the white tissue.
Then hang it up to dry.

Make a frame from black
sugar paper. First fold a
square of paper into four.

Then fold it from
corner to corner.

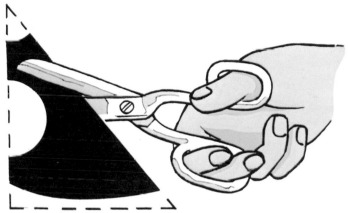

Draw a pattern on the folded paper and cut sections out as shown. Be careful to leave some of either folded edges uncut.

Experiment with newspaper to find your favourite designs. When unfolded you will find you have a regular pattern.

Stick the pattern onto the
coloured kitchen tissue.

Cut away the tissue paper around
the black pattern. Hang your design
by a thread or stick lightly to a
window.

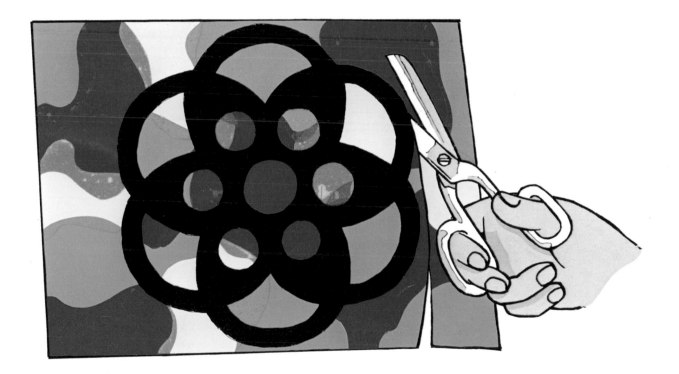

MONSTER

Simple animals, figures and many other things can be made with egg boxes, although the plastic variety are more difficult to work with.

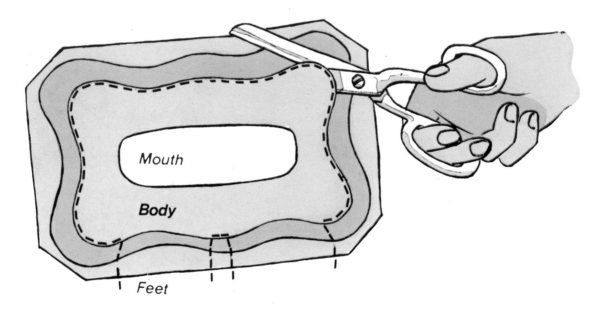

To make an eggbox monster cut off the top of an eggbox and follow the dotted lines above with your scissors.

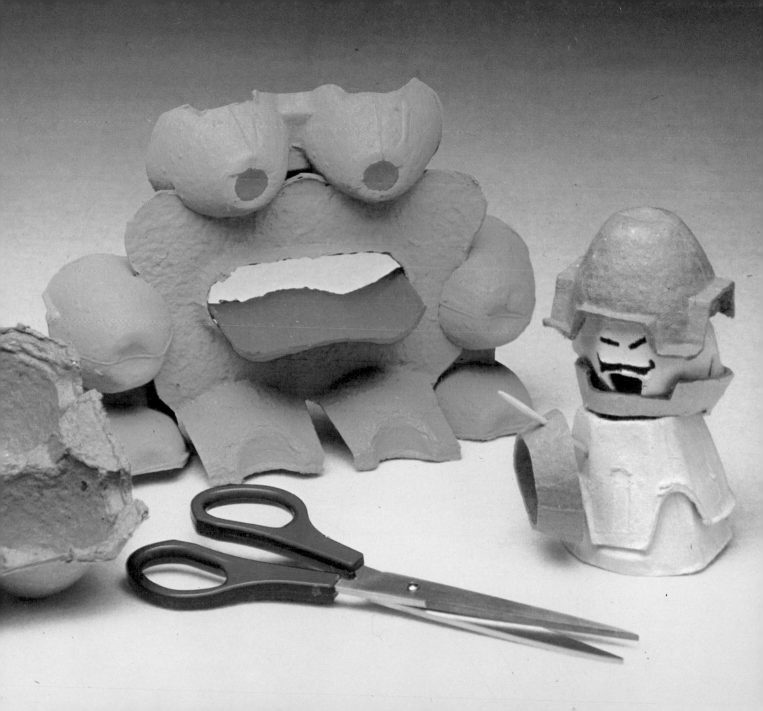

Cut up the bottom of the eggbox as shown below. Follow the dotted lines.

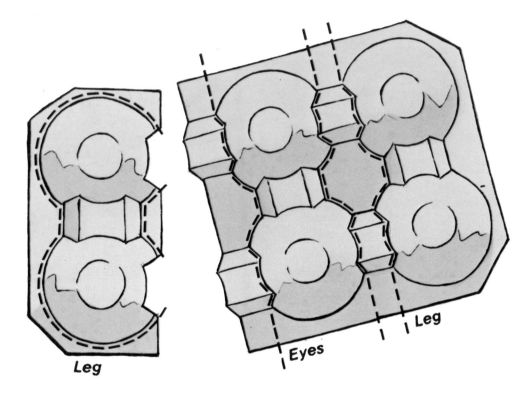

Leg

Eyes

Leg

These pieces make the eyes and legs.

With the edges trimmed, cut slots in the
eyes and legs as shown here.

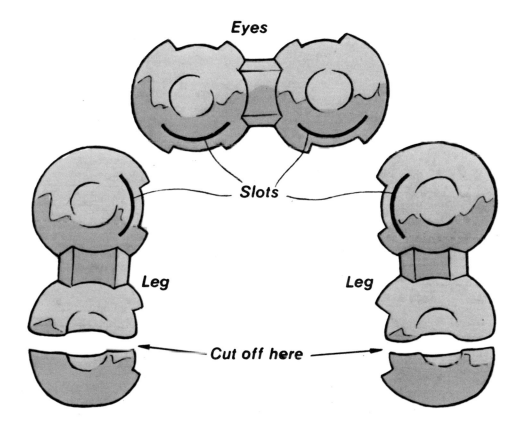

Eyes

Slots

Leg   **Leg**

← ----- **Cut off here** ----- →

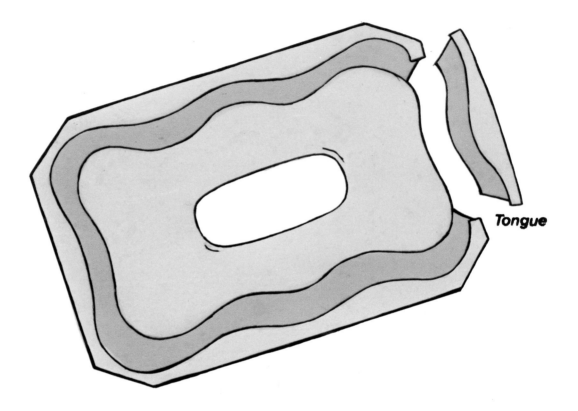

Tongue

To make a tongue, cut off the end of an eggbox lid.

Slot the eyes and legs onto the body. Push the tongue through from the back.

Now paint the monster with poster paint.

CHINESE SOLDIER

You need 2 different types of eggbox to make a Chinese soldier.

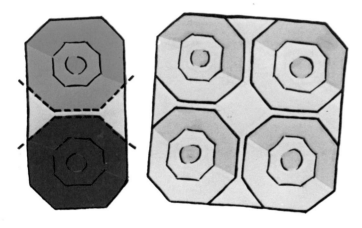

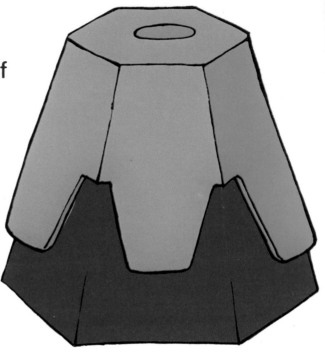

One make of eggbox has compartments shaped like smooth cones, the other has more angular shaped compartments. Cut the angular eggbox as shown above. Cut pieces from one section and place one on top of the other for the body. Do not colour yours until the model is complete.

28

Cut a third section from the angular eggbox for the head. Cut out a piece for the mouth and draw in the eyes and the moustache with a felt tip pen.

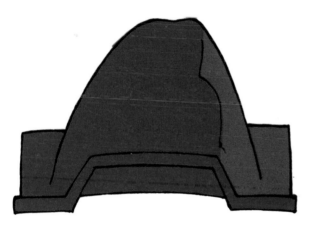

Cut a section from the cone-shaped eggbox and trim round the bottom. This makes the hat.

Cut another section from the cone-shaped eggbox and cut off the top. This makes the collar.

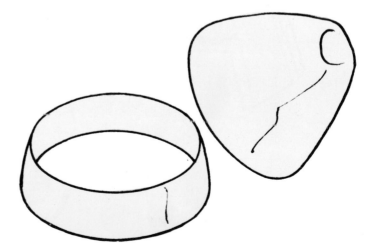

Cut a piece from the collar and fit the collar to the base. Cut slots in the head and fold the bottom of the head inwards as shown below.

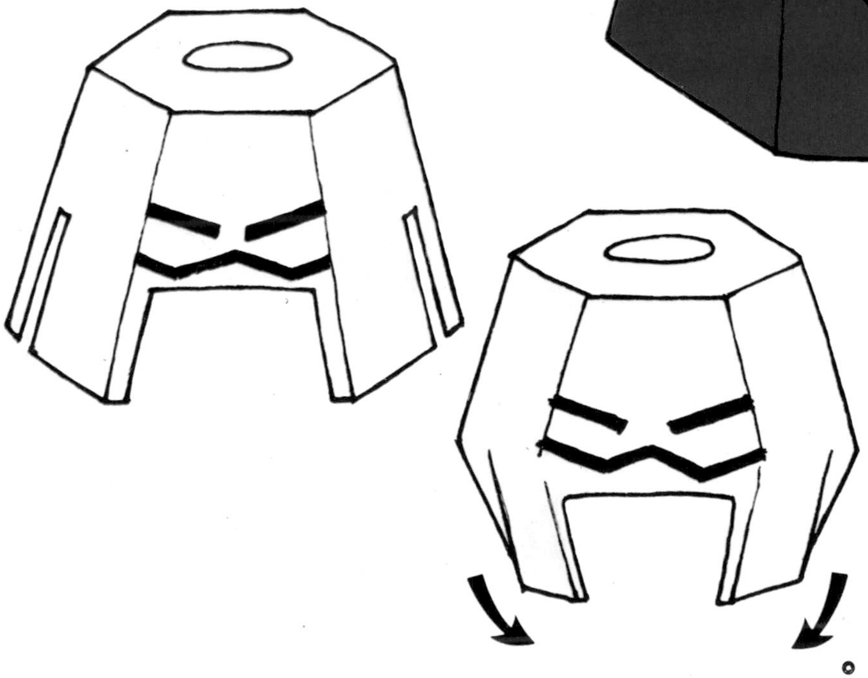

Fit the head into the
collar. Put the hat on
the head.

Trim another cone
from the cone-shaped
eggbox and cut off
the top. This makes the
shield. Push a cocktail
stick through the
shield and into the
body.

Your Chinese soldier
is now ready to paint.

BLOCK PRINTS

Cut a pattern from card. You can make a small picture from card shapes like the one shown here, or make a pattern from squares and circles, etc.

Stick your pattern together onto a
wooden block or a piece of card.

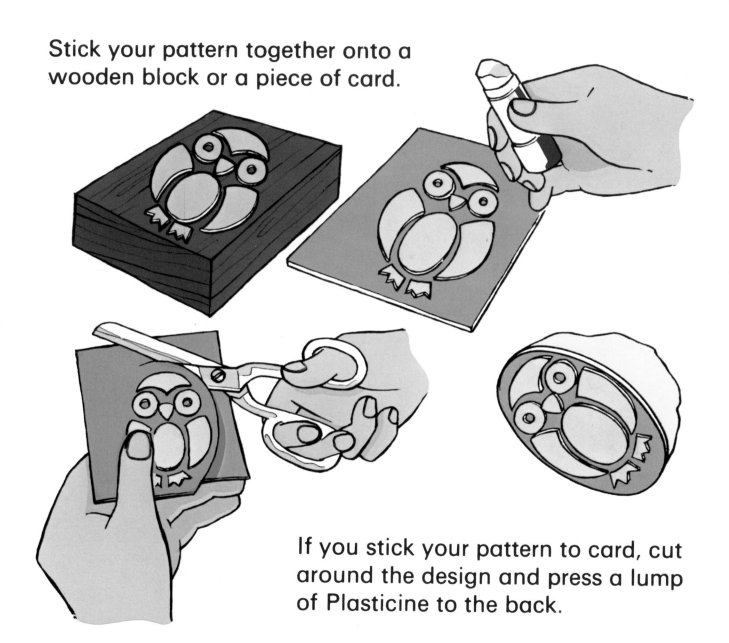

If you stick your pattern to card, cut
around the design and press a lump
of Plasticine to the back.

Paint the printing block with poster paint or powder paint. Add a little washing-up liquid to stop the paint from drying too quickly. Press the block onto a sheet of paper.

Re-paint the block each time you print. You can make a nice effect with a repeated pattern if you print over strips of paper. Remove after printing.

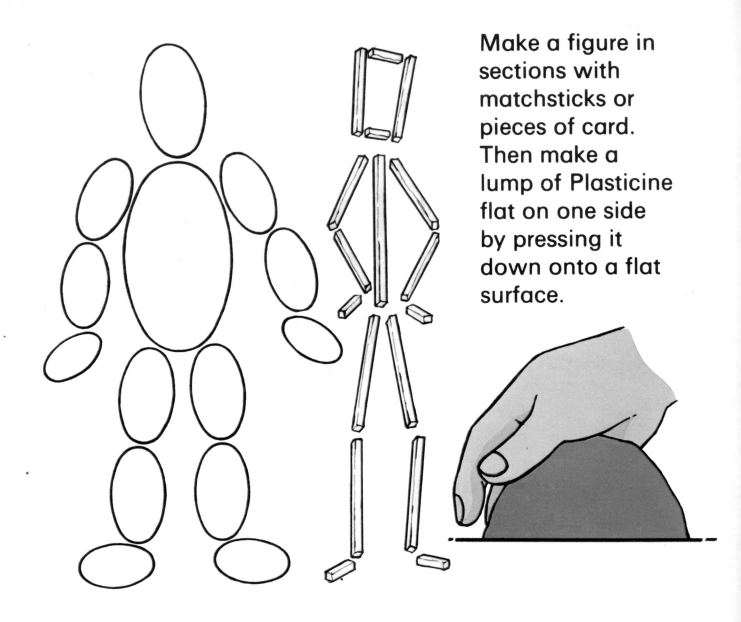

Make a figure in
sections with
matchsticks or
pieces of card.
Then make a
lump of Plasticine
flat on one side
by pressing it
down onto a flat
surface.

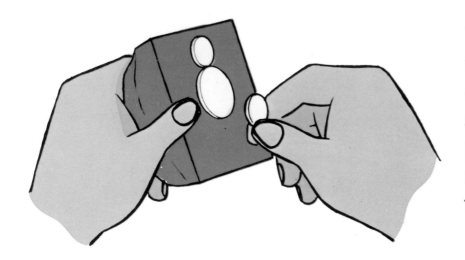

Trim the edge of the Plasticine to a rectangular shape. Press the pieces of card or matchsticks into the flat surface.

Make a print by painting the block in the same way as in 'block printing'. Move an arm or a leg between each print.

With these movable prints you can make an animated picture. Cut two strips of paper twice as wide as your block.

Make a print on each by lining up the block with the edge of the paper. Make the figure move as shown for the second sheet.
Staple the two pieces together. Flip the top piece up and down and your figure will move. Now make more action pictures for a flip book.

EDGE PRINTS

Paint the edge of a piece of card and press it onto a sheet of paper. Try using different types of card, e.g. corrugated for a different effect.

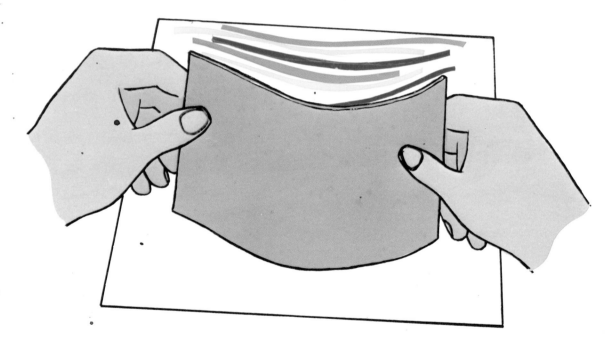

Bend the card to make curves, or fold it to make angles. You can print rectangles from the end of a matchbox, or circles from bottle tops.

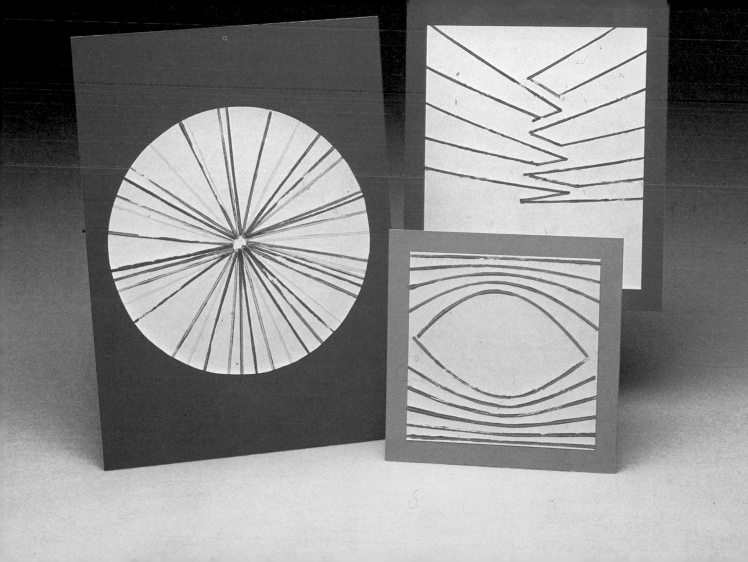

TRANSFER AND MONO PRINTS

Squeeze about one inch of water-based printing ink onto a flat surface such as Formica. Roll out the ink with a roller to an even film.

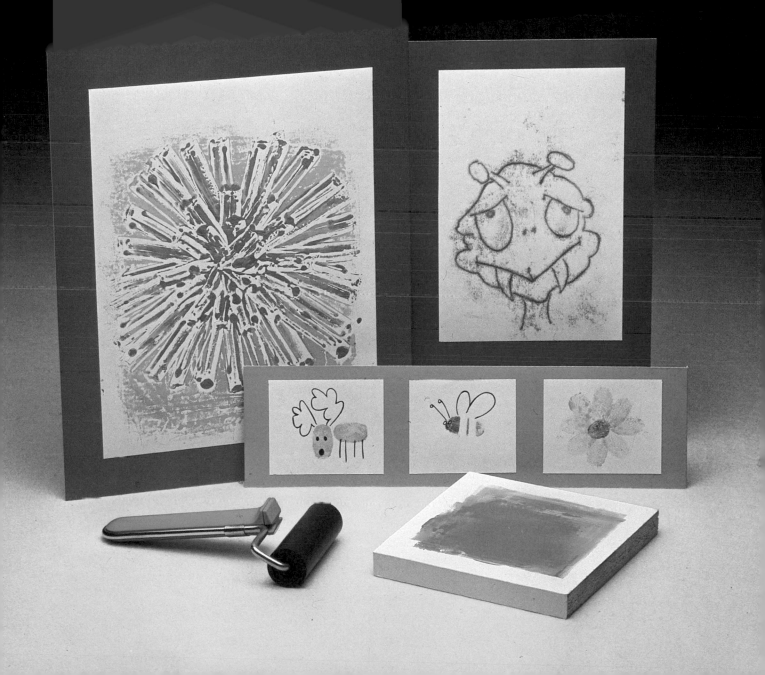

Draw a picture or cut one out from a magazine.
To make your monoprint put a piece of clean paper
over the film of ink. Place the picture on top and
trace over it in pencil.

You can rub in
areas of shading
with your finger.
Now lift off the
finished print.

For transfer prints roll out the ink
as before and draw a picture
or pattern into the ink film.

Make patterns with a pencil, pieces of card or
anything that will remove or scrape away the ink.
You can even try dabbing the ink with a sponge.

Carefully place a sheet of paper over your
design. Hold it in place with one hand
and rub over it with a soft cloth.
Lift off the paper.

Try making prints with two or
more colours together.

FINGER PRINTS

Press your fingers onto the inked flat surface and then onto paper. Make patterns, animals and figures by adding a few pen lines.

Use strips of paper to mask out areas. You can also make patterns with the roller. Just ink it up and see what designs you can make.

47

WAX TRANSFER

Rub a wax crayon over some greaseproof paper. Use several different colours.

Place a clean sheet of paper onto a hard, flat surface. Place the sheet of greaseproof paper coloured side down, on top. On top of this place a drawing, tracing or a picture from a magazine.

Draw over the picture with biro. Rub in areas of colour with the blunt end of a pen. Lift and see results.

You can also cover the greaseproof paper with a white wax crayon. Make your drawing, then paint the paper with a sponge.

Where you have pressed through the paper the transferred wax will not be coloured by the paint.

MASKS AND STENCILS

Fold a piece of card in
half and cut out a
shape or design.

You can use the holes in
the card as well as the
shapes you have cut out.

You can make a picture
in a number of different
ways. Dip the bristles
of a toothbrush into
some paint. Flick the
bristles with your thumb.

Or use a piece of sponge
to dab the paint on. Use
powder paint or make
chalk dust with chalk and
sandpaper and apply with
a pad of cotton wool.

SCREEN PRINTING

Screen printing is another way of using
masks. Pin a piece of net curtain to
a piece of plywood or cork tile.

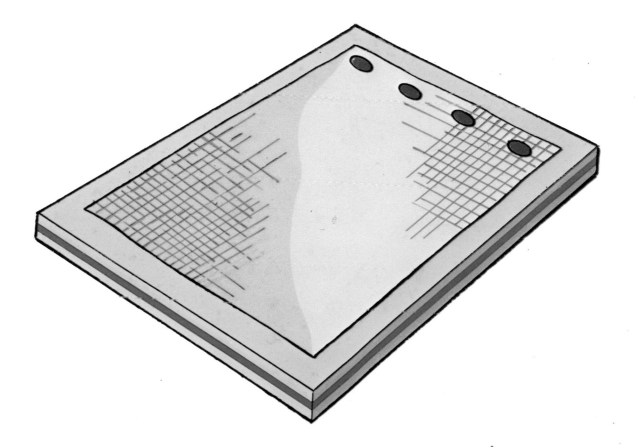

Make a pattern on the screen by sticking shapes
cut from sticky back plastic onto the other side
of the screen, or by painting a picture with PVA glue.
Put a sheet of plastic under the screen before you
paint on the glue. Do not remove it until the glue
is dry.

Mask off
all areas where
you do not want
the paint to go through.

You can make your screen print by dabbing on paint
with a sponge or flicking paint with a toothbrush.
Or you can squeeze out water-based printing ink
along the top of the screen and spread the ink
down towards you with a stiff card.

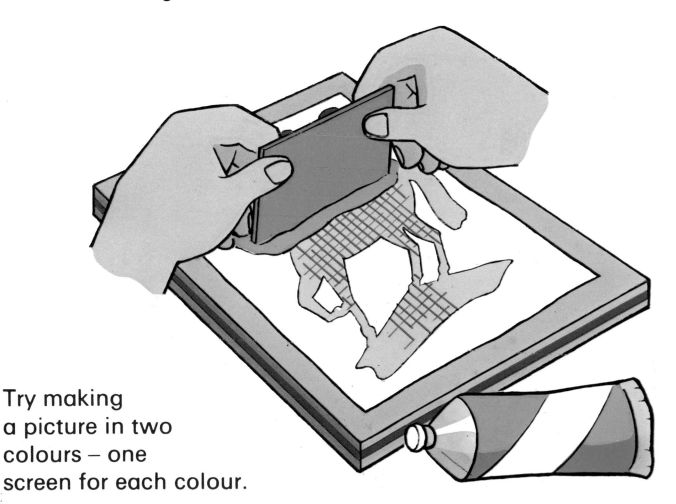

Try making
a picture in two
colours – one
screen for each colour.

SNAKES
To make a snake cut from card 10 of each triangle A and 5 each of B and C

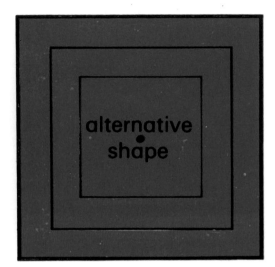

alternative shape

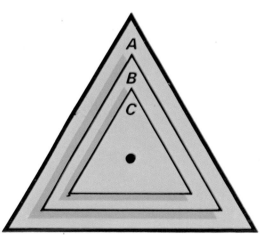

A
B
C

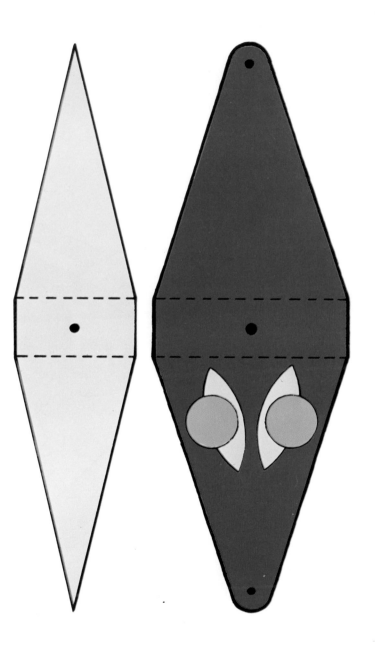

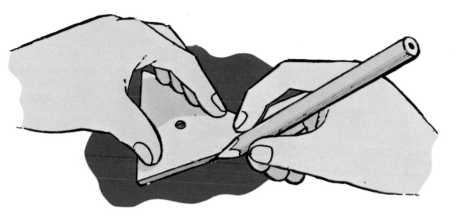

Stick coloured
paper to card
before cutting out
shapes or cut card
first and colour
with felt tip pens.

Trace and cut out one
triangle of each size.
Use these shapes to
draw round until you
have enough. Cut
out triangles and
make a hole
through the
centre of each
with a nail.

59

Trace or draw the head
and tail onto card and cut
out. Score along the lines
to be folded with a biro.
Stick on coloured paper
and trim edges with
scissors.

Or colour head and tail
with felt tip pen.

Stick coloured paper
shapes on for eyes.

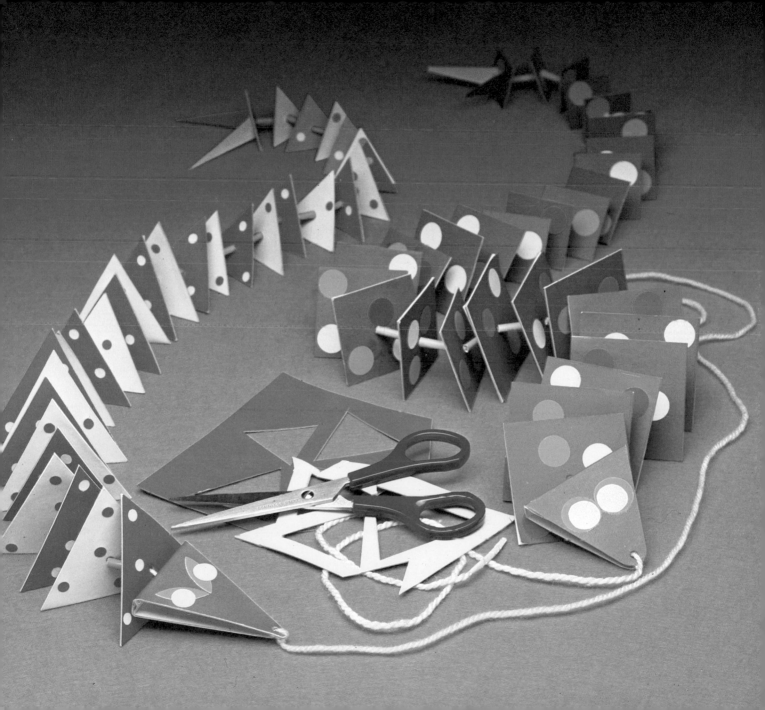

Take some scissors and some plastic drinking straws. Cut 20 pieces each 15 mm long. Cut a length of wool 600 mm long and tie a knot in one end.

Wrap some sticky tape round the other end to make threading easier. Thread the tail onto the wool, then a piece of straw, next a triangle.

Continue in this way until you have used up all the pieces. Last of all thread the wool through the nead and tie a knot.

You can make snakes out of other shapes. Try squares or circles.

FISH MOBILES

Put a piece of white 2 ply
kitchen paper on top of
several sheets of newspaper.

Dab ink or poster paint onto the
kitchen paper with a large paintbrush
or sponge. If you like you can make
the paper damp first.

Hang the kitchen paper up to dry. Bend a piece of wire into the outline of a fish. When the paper is dry, cut off one of the

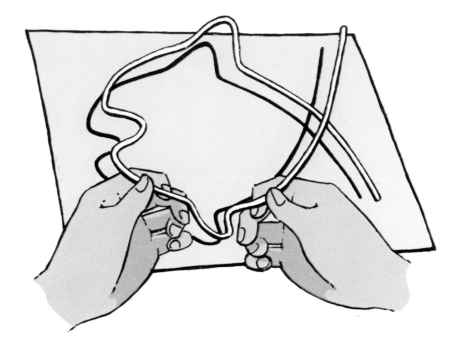

edges where the paper is joined together and separate the two layers of paper. Rub over one layer with a glue stick.

Place the fish on
the paper. Starting
at the joined edge,
press the two
layers together.

When the fish is
dry trim round
the fish 5 mm
from wire.
Make a small hole
and with cotton
hang your fish
where the light
shines through it.

MOPPETS
Use these shapes to trace
onto card to make the
features for these
funny creatures.

Cover the wooden handle of a
dishmop with coloured paper.
Glue in place.

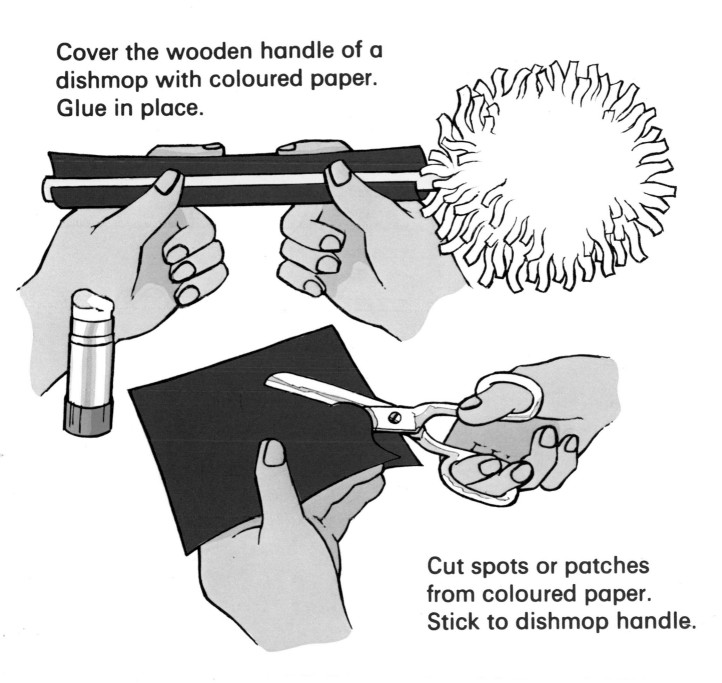

Cut spots or patches
from coloured paper.
Stick to dishmop handle.

Stick some coloured paper
onto a piece of card.
Make the body in any
shape or size you wish.

Stick some spots on the
body to match the dish-
mop handle. Make holes
in the body with a nail,
about 10 mm apart.

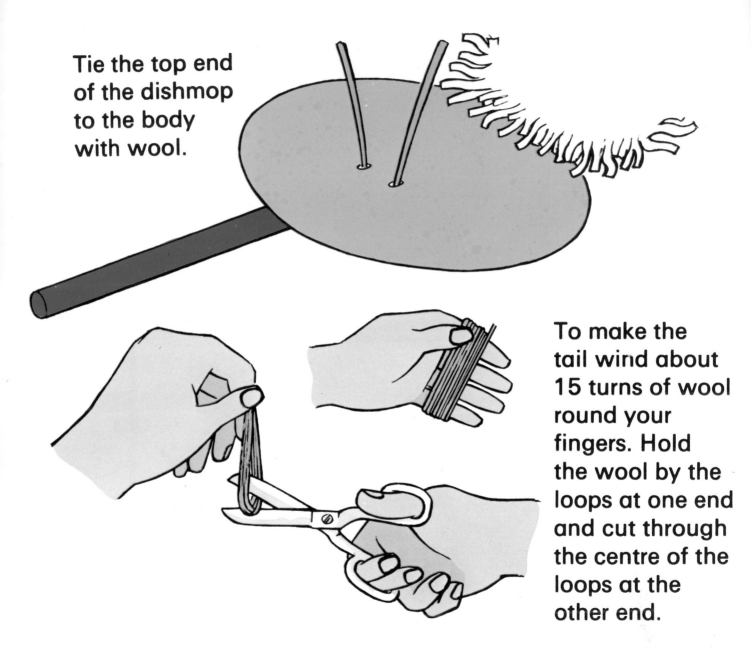

Tie the top end
of the dishmop
to the body
with wool.

To make the
tail wind about
15 turns of wool
round your
fingers. Hold
the wool by the
loops at one end
and cut through
the centre of the
loops at the
other end.

Tie the tail to the
body with the ends
of wool left after
tying the body to
the dishmop handle.

Stick the beak and
eyes to the mophead.
Stick the feet and
wings to the body.

73

WOOLLIES

To make the eyes wind
some wool round three
fingers ten times.
Slip the wool off your
fingers. Tie in centre.

Make three
bunches of
wool for each
eye.

Make a hook at one end of a piece of plastic covered garden wire 80 mm long. Push the wire through the ties in the middle of the bunches of wool. Push each bunch up the hook. Squeeze the hook tight and trim the eye.

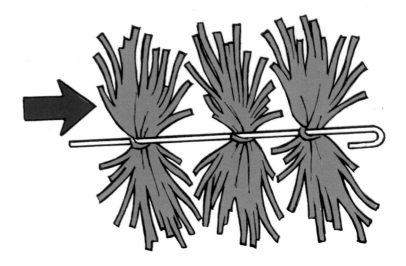

Make three more
bunches of wool and
slip them onto the
same wire. Make a
hook at the other
end and push the
bunches up to it.
Squeeze the hook
together and trim
the eye as before.

Make the nose in the same
way as an eye on a piece of
wire about 200 mm long.

Choose a different colour
wool for the head and
make bunches longer than
those for the eyes by
winding the wool round
four fingers this time.
You will need about
ten big bunches.
Push four of them onto the wire up to the nose.

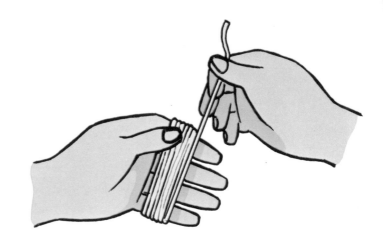

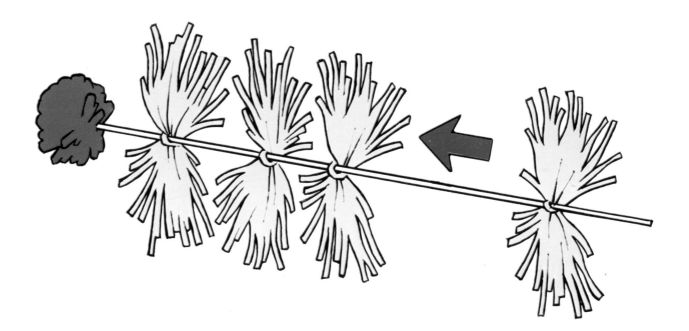

Wind the wire with the eyes on tightly round the wire going through the head until the eyes are level with the rest of the head.

Push the eyes up towards the nose. Push the remaining bunches for the head onto the wire and trim until you are happy with the shape. If you want to make the head bigger add more bunches of wool.

The body needs to be 80 mm wide. If your hand is not wide enough, make bunches in the same way as before but tie them through one end and cut the loops at the other.

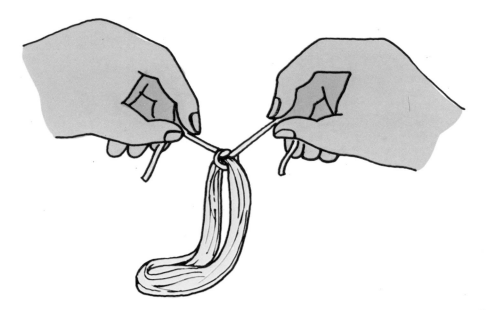

Make bunches for body until you are satisfied the body is long enough. Make 4 or 5 bunches in a different colour for the tail and slide them onto wire. Bend wire behind tail.

Push the wool back and bend the wire
into a hook. Cut the wire 10 mm from
the bend. Push the bunches up onto the
hook.

Now you can spread
out the body and tail.

To make legs wind bunches of
wool the same size as for the
eyes. Cut a wire 180 mm long
and make a hook at one end.
Make a leg at each end of the
wire.

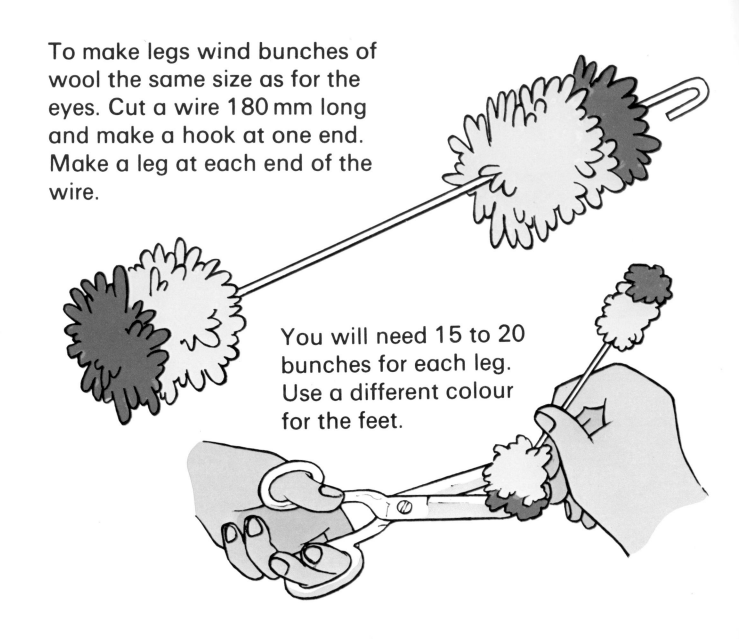

You will need 15 to 20
bunches for each leg.
Use a different colour
for the feet.

Push the bunches of wool back from the head and attach the front legs in the same way as the eyes, by winding them round the body wire. Attach the back legs between the tail and the body. Spread out the wool to cover the wires.

If you are going to give the woolly animal to a very small child use wool through the body, eyes and nose instead of wire.

GOLD COINS. Start by tracing these designs.

Draw or trace the design of a coin onto the rough side of a piece of card. Use a compass to draw the circles. Paint PVA glue thickly along the lines of the coin design.

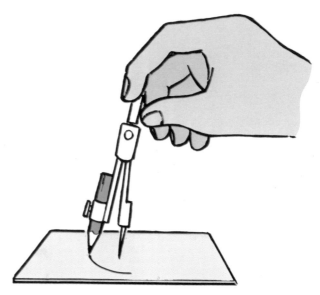

Leave on a flat surface to dry.

When the glue is
dry paint over the
design with gold or
silver poster paint.
You will need at
least two coats
to cover the glue.
Leave the paint
to dry between
coats.

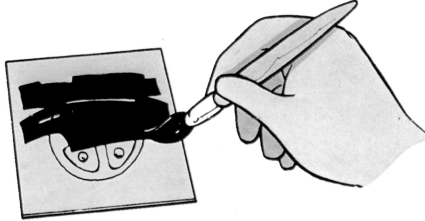

When the gold
paint is dry,
mix some black
paint and cover
the design
completely.

Before the black
paint dries, press
a sheet of
newspaper over
the coin. Rub the
paper with your
finger.

Lift the paper and
you will find that
some of the paint has
been removed. You
can remove more by
rubbing the paper
again.

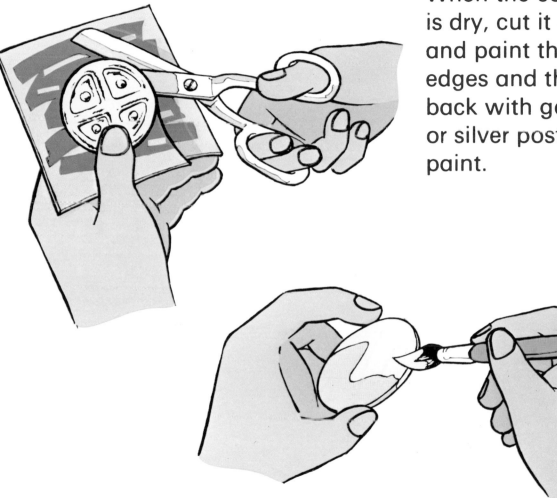

When the coin
is dry, cut it out
and paint the
edges and the
back with gold
or silver poster
paint.

JEWELLERY. Here are some pendant designs that you can make in the same way as the coins.

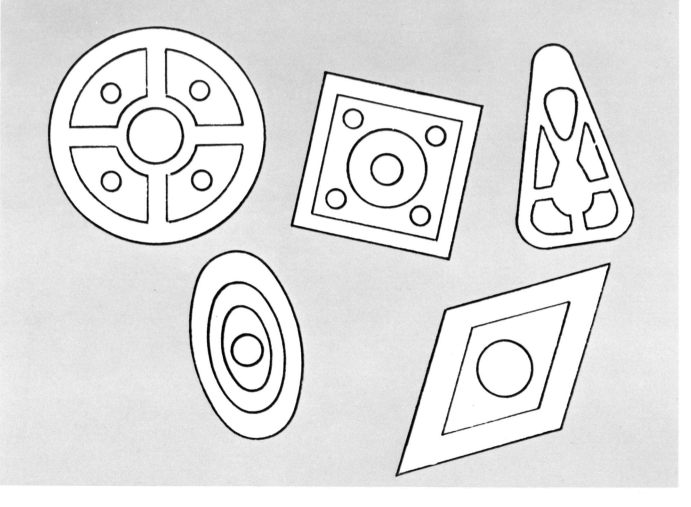

Cut a strip of card
about 4 cm wide.
Wrap the strip
round your wrist,
mark the length
and cut the card
to fit your wrist.
Make a note of
this length for
making other
bracelets.

Draw and paint a design
on the bracelet in the
same way as the coins.

Decorate your design
with jewels by sticking
on beads, lentils or split
peas.

To fasten the bracelet
put paper fasteners at
the ends of the strip and
join the bracelet by winding
wool between them. Stick
Sellotape on the back to stop
the fasteners from digging
into your wrist.

Bracelets can also be
made in sections joined
by lengths of wool.

Necklaces can be made
from string and pasta
tubes. Paint the pasta
tubes different colours.

You can stick seeds or lentils to
the painted pasta with PVA glue.

Necklaces can also be made
by threading pendants onto
wool. Coloured straws cut to
length, with a paperclip or
hairclip in the end can also
be used.

TREASURE CHEST
Find two boxes the same size,
one for the top and one
for the bottom.

Mark out and cut a strip of card that will fit around the inside of one of the boxes and will stand up about 1 cm from the top of the box. Glue the strip in place.

When the glue is dry paint the inside
and outside of both boxes brown.
Leave brush strokes in the paint
to make it look like wood.

Make some more cardboard strips to cover the box like this. The best way to do this is shown on the next page.

Cut out strips, then use clothes pegs
to hold them in place while you mark
and fold them. Do not glue in place yet.

When you have all the strips
cut and folded, paint designs on
them as you did for the coins.
When you are painting the
strips black, paint them in
sections so that you can rub
off the excess paint
before it dries.

Stick the strips onto the chest with double-sided
Sellotape or by using a glue stick.

Using these designs, make a lock and two hinges in the same way as you made the coins.

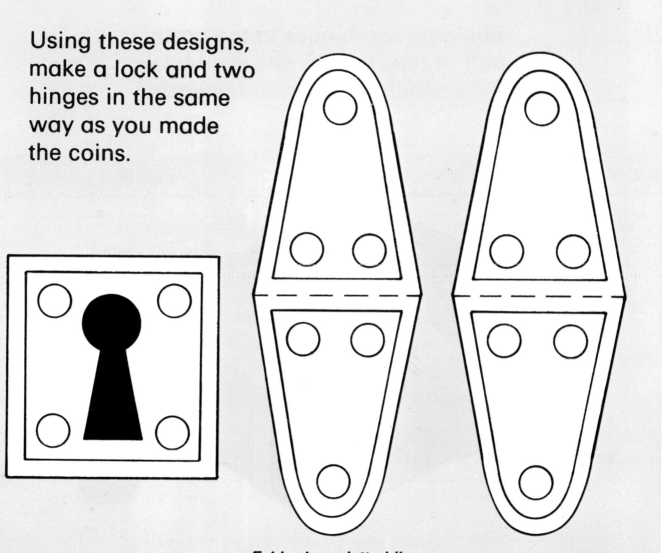

Folds along dotted line.

Stick the two hinges to the bottom half of the chest as shown. Make more secure with paper fasteners.

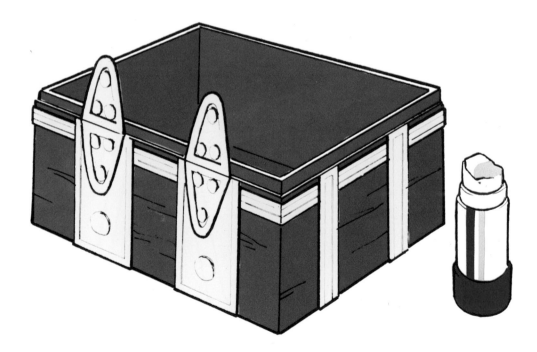

Put the top of the chest on and attach the hinges as before.

Glue the lock to the front of the chest.

GOLDEN PICTURES

Here is a design
using fairly
simple shapes.

Trace or draw the
design onto a piece
of card and cut out
the shapes. Stick
them in position on
a piece of flat card.

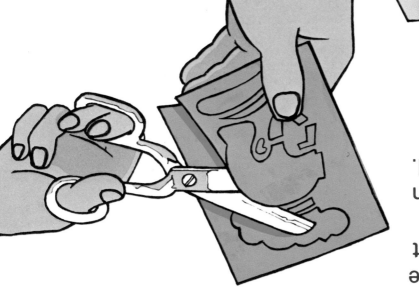

Allow glue to dry.
Paint the whole
card black.

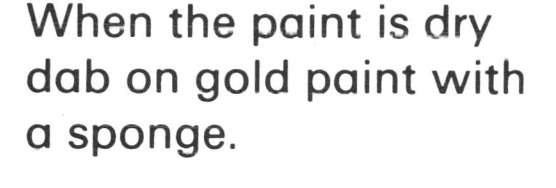

When the paint is dry
dab on gold paint with
a sponge.

Try displaying your
pictures on different
backgrounds, such as wood,
coloured paper or rough
material such as hessian.